SEX IN YOUR POCKET

How to get More Dates with Women on Dating Apps

By

Brady PUA

This book is dedicated to:

Technology. For connecting me to women, so I can connect with them.

Table of Contents

Introduction

You have, in your presence right now, the ability to drastically change your life forever. You have the power to chase every dream that you have ever imagined of achieving. Right in front of you, is the ability to have any girl you want.

I am not talking about this book either. I am talking about You. This shit already exists inside of you. Some of you have realized this already, and some are hearing it for the first time. And this is not some meta-physical bullshit I am saying to you.

It is real. I remember when I first realized this. I was on a morning walk, desperately trying to cut my body fat to sub 10%. I thought hot women only liked guys in amazing shape. I was already in decent shape, why were the women not flocking to me?

Sure, being in shape helped a bit, but it was not the results I had dreamed of yet. Little did I know at that point, I was doing this shit way wrong. What makes women attracted to men I thought? Hmmm, a low body fat percentage and a sense of humor I thought.

Oh, fuck was I wrong. But I did not know it yet. I did not know it until I downloaded a book on seduction.

I became hooked on the book, studying my ass off and digesting every word. Then I bought another book to learn more, deepen my knowledge until I finally realized, it was test time. Time to put the shit I was studying to use.

Guess what, the shit worked! I was so nervous too. I had no idea what to expect. Some of the concepts I learned about were wild to me: can I actually get away with saying this shit to a girl?

Yes! That was the whole purpose. Even the many times it did not work, the lessons learned were more valuable to me than any chapter I read. This is the ultimate concept that I want you to realize.

Sure, I am selling books here. To be honest with you, at this current price point, I am making around $3 per book sold. This is before taxes. Not nearly enough to be a millionaire from this shit any time soon.

Divide that into the hours spent writing and researching and I am quite fucked. I can barely buy a happy hour beer in my city from my profits of your purchase. Boo hoo.

Regardless, I want to spread this knowledge to you. I want to give you the recipe for your own success. That is what this book will do. I will always recommend the books that jumpstarted me in to Pick-up, however this is a refreshed, 21st century book.

Maybe you bought this book because you want to have more sex. Maybe you bought it because you want a girlfriend. Maybe both. Whatever your reason, the knowledge in this book will bring you a lot closer to that goal. It will instruct on what women will look for in a man, and how to build your online profile to reflect those qualities. This will lead you to more matches, more conversations, and more dates. I will also provide you with what to say to turn those matches into dates. Most importantly, this book teaches you how the overall correct attitude you will need when talking to beautiful women. Having that alone is worth so much more than a few pick-up lines.

Again, this book will help, but it is not the answer to everything. The answer is here, but it lies in you. It is in you to act. To execute the philosophies in this book, to approach more, to start more conversations with beautiful women. The action is on you. I can lead you to more gorgeous women, but I am not talking her in to letting you put your dick in her for you.

Now go and learn! Then, put it to use and start talking to women! If you enjoy what this book offers, please check out my other content at www.bradypua.com and email me any questions or success stories you have. Email: bradyPUA@gmail.com

PART I: Overview of the Five Main Attraction Switches

"If you can convey those five key DHVs in your stories, then a woman is going to feel attraction for you"

- Mystery discussing next level of game on YouTube.

Are you aware of the five main attraction switches? If not, no worries. I have dedicated part one of this book to an overview of the five main attraction switches.

The attraction switches that I discuss in the following chapter are all extremely important concepts to comprehend when you want to increase your success with women. Understand that this topic, and even each attraction switch, could have its own chapters or books as that is how powerful this concept is. There is plenty of material one can find online regarding attraction switches and I will be completing more in-depth material on them for future blog posts and books. I will update this section of the book when that new content becomes available. For now, you can check out my site at   to see what else I have released.

Note, most of these ideas and concepts belong to Mystery. Every Pick-up Artist who has followed his work, like myself, will offer their own variations and tweaks based on their experiences; however, Mystery, in my opinion, is one of the most influential people in all of seduction. If you have not heard of him, it would be beneficial to you to check out his work as well.

Part I of this book will give you a high-level overview of what women are attracted to in a man.

Chapter One: Attraction Switches

Imagine a light switch that is down in the off position. When you do something that a woman finds attractive, imagine that switch being flipped up and turned on. This is an attraction switch. Every man and woman have attraction switches; however, what they consist of differs by gender. Men feel attraction when a hot, young lady walks by with big tits and a great ass. She is checking off our attraction switches relating to reproduction: we want to have sex with her. Women have attraction switches as well, but they are more closely related to the survival value a male has.

Below, I list and discuss the five main attraction switches:

- Leader of Men

- Successful Risk Taking

- Willingness to Emote

- Protector of Loved Ones

- Pre-Selection

Please note, these are discussed throughout this book as "attraction switches" but, in my opinion, they all add up to an Attraction Score. I talk about this Attraction Score in depth in my other works but, for now, just imagine a 1-100 rating system in a ladies' head for each separate attraction switch. Every time you flip one of the switches, your score goes up for that attraction switch. A score of 1 is the lowest and a score of 100 is the most attracted a woman could be to that quality in you. All men do not start a 1 either. Every guy has a different starting score for that woman and these scores are constantly being updated depending on how the woman feels about you. Keep this in mind as you read through these chapters and, more-importantly, as you interact with women in your life.

Also note, I only discuss the five *main* attraction switches. There are a hell of a fucking lot more such as Social Intelligence switches and Disinterest switches, but it is a common understanding among the pick-up community that the ones above are the five main switches. I talk about other switches further in my blog at www.bradyPUA.com. Yes, I will be plugging my other shit throughout this book, get used to it.

Leadership

Women crave a man who has amazing leadership qualities. In fact, society craves this in general. Being a leader is about bringing people together, uniting them, and then moving them forward with them for the better of all.

When you are interacting with a woman, you need to lead. Say the word "leader" out loud right now. Leader. You are almost saying the words "lead her" when you do. Sure, women are independent and can survive fine without you, however nothing is more unattractive to a woman than a guy who bends and breaks at her every command. A guy needs to stay strong and demonstrate he is a leader at every step of the way.

This can be done with simple actions. Are you picking her up for the date? Did you plan it out? Never ever ask a girl what she wants to do on the first date. You need to lead and show her that you know how to plan and have a good time.

You need to take charge with a woman. Sometimes this means doing things that are uncomfortable, but you have the courage to do them anyway! Reach to hold her hand, tell her you want to kiss her, or even lean in and do it!

Nice guys always seem to wait for the woman to feel comfortable before they make a move (See note below). Or, they always wait for the lady to make the first move. Scratch all those ideas and start making the first moves yourself. Imagine that it is always going amazing and continue to escalate throughout the dates. Escalate the conversation, escalate your physical touch, and keep things moving forward, but in the direction that you want.

Note: Almost all women will have sex on the first date, if the guy is right for them. If you can demonstrate you are the exact man she wants/needs, she will let herself succumb to you in every way.

Here are some examples from women on that demonstrate a man being an attractive leader:

- Picks her up for the date and doesn't ask "what do you want to do?"; he already has something planned

- Controls the conversation so there are no dull moments, awkward moments

- Knows the appropriate moments to escalate physically

- Takes charge

- Demonstrates being the Alpha Male in a group of guys

The examples above provide a general idea on how to act to demonstrate what it means to be a leader to a woman. In the following chapters, you will see routines and stories that I tell which will show this quality in a detailed manner.

Successful Risk Taking

Would you jump out of an airplane? Have you broken any laws? Would you risk your life to save the damsel in distress?

Successful risk taking is an attraction switch that can be demonstrated in an abundant amount of ways. Think about every action movie where the hero gets the girl in the end. It is usually because the guy is risking his life to save others, or for the good of all people. This type of behavior is extremely attractive to women.

One of the ways to convey successful risk taking is to have that "Bad boy" edge about you. Women want a guy who is a "bad boy" but also a softy as well. Someone who can be exciting, take her on a thrill ride, but still make her feel safe enough to take home and introduce to her parents.

The action movies of Hollywood take this attraction switch to the extreme, however think about romantic comedies you have seen before. In 10 <u>Things I Hate About You</u>, Heath Ledgers' character prances around the bleachers outside of school, serenading his female interest (Julia Styles) over the PA system speakers. School security is called on him, he receives a detention, but this is another example of successful risk taking.

Now, of course you do not need to be Bruce Willis or Heath Ledger, flip this switch. Like the other switches, this can be flipped simply by telling a small story of a time you took a risk, showing a picture of something you did before, or demonstrating it live on a small scale (really powerful).

Do you have any stories of any fears that you recently faced? Any story where you can talk about living on the edge of your own cliff and jumping off to take a chance. For me, fuck heights, I am not a fan of them. However, I subtly show a successful risk-taking quality by showing a fear that I face in the below story (routine).

My office is in one of the tallest buildings in the downtown area of my city. Still to this day riding the elevator can cause me some fear and panic. As buildings do not usually topple over randomly and elevator accidents are few and far between, the chances of me being injured from my fear of heights are almost zero. To this day though, when a woman asks me where I work, I tell them, but I be sure to include my fear of heights in my description as well. I continue the conversation with a short story about how my fear of heights lead me to become the Emergency Coordinator for my floor and now I am trained to act in case of an emergency. I even make fun of the orange vest and small cone that sit on my desk to alert other office dwellers that I am the man in case of an emergency. I talk about how it takes forever to evacuate the building during the various drills that we have so if anything were to happen, I am pretty sure we would all be fucked.

I am sure to finish the story with the fact that on windy days, the building sways and moves. I am descriptive about seeing the water in my bottle swish around and hearing the creeks of the support beams behind the walls. I even have a video on my phone that I show of the doors opening and closing on their own during an especially windy day that I use if she is demonstrating high interest in the conversation.

This story does two things: first, I am demonstrating the leader of men quality as I talk about being the Emergency Floor Coordinator, and second, I am showing that every day I take a risk going to work in the office. It is subtle, but it is there. Sometimes subtlety is the approach you need as you do not want to come off too strong or too bragging. If you start talking about how you jumped out of an airplane or pushed an elderly lady out of the way of traffic, it is fine, but you can easily overdo it as well. I like to flip the successful risk taking with a small story, such as the one above, that displays a little vulnerability as well. Be careful here as that can be overdone as well.

Women that I have talked to regarding the attraction switch of Successful Risk Taking usually have this switch running closely with the Leader of Men attraction switch. They can be quick actions that a female finds attractive, or character traits that a man displays that are attractive. Examples that have been given to me are things such as:

- If walking on a sidewalk, walk on the side of the lady that is closest to the traffic. You are taking the small risk of being hit if a car jumps a curb

- Leading her to a closed off area to sneak into a venue

- Taking the lead to drive or calling a taxi if you have been out drinking

- Taking career risks or financial risks and coming out successful in the end

As you can see from the above examples, these some of the actions or traits that a woman would find extremely attractive. See the appendix for some other demonstration of higher value stories that will show successful risk taking.

Willingness to Emote

A man with well-timed vulnerabilities is sexy to a woman. Sure, she wants you to be a tough-as-nails man's man, but showing the correct level of emotion will ensure to her that you have the caring side that she needs in a mate.

Women need to make sure that you will be there on an emotional level for them. When she comes home after a hard day, can she look to you to be her rock? Can you be the type of guy to listen to her and understand how she is feeling? Do you have any unnatural anger or emotional issues deep inside of you?

These are all cues that women will search for in a man. Sure, she thinks you are cute and a leader, but if you turn into an animal when things do not go your way, it is a major red flag. She needs to know you are not a psychopath and capable of feeling a wide range of emotions. Fucking lighten up bro.

This does not mean that you need to feel sad and cry on her shoulder every day, nor does this mean that you cannot show anger either. You must show all these emotions; however, you must show them at proper levels. I am upset when my favorite sports team loses a game. I do not rip my TV off the wall and smash it because of the game. When something sad happens, be sad! Be strong enough to not fall into a lengthy depression over it though.

Let your woman lean on you and show her the support she needs. Most of the time, this can be conveyed simply by being a good listener and understanding how she is feeling. Also, if she is being truly unreasonable, be a man and call her out over that shit. Don't take it from her. These are all examples of a man that is showing normal emotional programming.

Women will be on the lookout for your emotional behavior. Be sure to express all emotions accurately and at the correct levels. This will help to bond her emotions to yours and raise her attraction towards you. Women are way more emotionally intelligent than men. More on this later.

Protector of Loved Ones

Thinking back to the tribal days of humans, males provided a necessary service to females: protection and security.

Women want to feel protected and secure around you. This can be demonstrated a tad by your physical attributes: do you look like someone who is strong and can be a protector? Like the other switches in this chapter, this is also demonstrated by your traits and actions as well.

You do not go looking for altercations, however, if one were to arise would she feel protected with you? Does she feel that you will be a great protector of your future children as well? Can she trust that you will be that security blanket for your family?

Do not go picking fights or putting you or her in danger to convey being a protector. You also do not need to have kids to show that you are able to protect a loved one. Sometimes I tell the story about the time that I took my 7-year-old nephew on a bro date around town. He lives in a rural area so crossing the streets in the downtown part of my busy suburb was new to him. I talk about how I taught him to look both ways while crossing the street, and how cute it was when we were holding hands and skipping across the intersections.

Any small story like the one above is an easy way to flip the switch. Remember, the subtler, the better. You do not want to be bragging about doing these things, you want them to come off as just a part of your character. When I am on a date with a girl and I have told her the story of taking my nephew out, I am always sure to grab her hand and tell her to look both ways at each intersection just as if I was teaching my nephew all over again. It is a funny little reminder of the protector of loved ones story and a subtle way to flip that switch again.

Provide the protection and security to your female and she will always find that part of you attractive. Be the man strong man inside and out, but display the cues that show you will defend the ones you love.

Pre-Selection

I saved Pre-selection for last because it is by far the most important one. The idea of pre-selection is based on the numerous studies of Mate Choice Copying amongst a variety of animals, including humans.

Mate choice copying is essentially the idea that the female gender will view a male as more attractive if he is observed already with a female. The idea is that the male has already been *pre-selected* by a female, therefore he must already have flipped all the other attraction switches to that female, i.e. he must be a good choice. The female would not be with him unless he has already demonstrated that he is a leader, he is a successful risk taker, he has shown her his normal emotional programming, and that he is a protector of his loved ones.

This is, by far, the most important attraction switch for men to utilize. By showing yourself with a female, you are already more than halfway to flipping the attraction switches on any female who observed you. There are some important things to consider, such as the attractiveness of the female you are with will play a role into how much attraction is given by pre-selection (if a female observer deems the female you are with as attractive as well, it is a bigger boost for you, and vice versa). Also, the interactions between you and the female you are with will matter such as being romantic with the female you are with is more attractive than arguing with her.

Having this switch flipped in a woman's mind will make the rest of the attraction building process immensely easier. Simple ways to flip this switch are:

- Being around a lot of women who are having fun, or you are romantically involved with

- Having pictures of yourself with a lot of attractive women around

- **Subtlety** talk about times that other women were attracted to you and the stories behind it (note this can be easy to exaggerate and over-convey, be sure to test your stories first)

- Wild sex stories that you tell, once you hit those topics of conversation

You will see examples how I convey pre-selection over the next few chapters. I am sure to use my pictures that I upload, as well as layering small pre-selection cues in my bio and conversation to be sure that this important attraction switch is flipped.

Chapter Summary

These are the five main attraction switches. Be sure to memorize them and know how to flip them in a girl's mind. You can easily do it with your conversations and actions. In any stories or routines that you build, be sure that you are flipping them while also being subtle about it to not convey bragging. This will keep your stories, and personality, believable.

Visualizing these switches being individually flipped is something I do when interacting with a female. It helps me to be sure that I am not using fluff talk all the time and I am constantly moving forward and escalating. With a little experience and assistance given in the next chapters, you too will soon be flipping these switches like the ultimate ladies' man.

PART II: Building the Perfect Profile

In this part we will focus on the two main parts of your online dating profile: pictures and bio.

Women are browsing on dating apps for many different reasons. Some are on there to promote their premium content. Some are on there to find true love. A lot of women are on them because they too busy to date, new to an area, and/or maybe they do not want to meet guys at bars anymore. They turn to technology to assist them in meeting people.

Another thing to consider, the mind state of a woman will vary when on these apps as well. Some will be swiping as more of a joke to laugh at the profiles, such as your current one. Sometimes they can be frustrated when swiping because any guy they match with is lame or just wants sex. Sometimes they are horny and simply want to have sex with an attractive guy (yes, this really happens).

Regardless of what a woman is looking for or how she feels, I want you to have a robust profile so the attraction starts to build as soon as your profile pops up. We want a woman to read our profile and have their feelings and emotions drawn to us! If we can accomplish this, we will already have a great start to the interaction, and the lady will be more accepting and inviting to your messages. This is the reality that we want to achieve.

Women want this as well. Maybe they are browsing the apps for a laugh, however, they also did not upload pictures of themselves and/or create a bio just to laugh at your profile. There is a little bit of hope there that someone will be intriguing to them, even if they only believe this a tiny bit. They would love it if you had an attractive profile, then followed that up with great conversation. They want to meet someone new and exciting. The truth is, they are pulling for you as well. Sure, they will test you and look for anything negative about your profile, but they actually want you to win. They want you to be the guy to sweep them off their feet and this book will allow you to do that.

Starting with your pictures, I will discuss what women look for in each one, which ones you should upload, and the various do's and don'ts when it comes to pictures of yourself. The tips that you need to know about how to visually represent yourself are all below. Pictures are worth a thousand words. You need to ensure that those words a flipping each attraction switch in the women that is viewing them.

Part II of this book will talk about how to build the best bio for your profile. So many things go into a great bio. This is your chance to convey a lot of personality in a little amount of space. Choose the characteristics in you that are the most attractive to woman and put them on full display here. I will teach you how to do all of that, and why this is my favorite part of the process.

Read on. Take notes. Let's meet some women!

Chapter Two: Pictures

Men who think they just need to upload the best-looking pictures of themselves are missing so much when it comes to building your profile. Let's do away with the up-close profile pics, the photoshopped or grainy face pics, and fuck off with those shirtless selfies. I am here to help you pick the best pictures to attract women and make them want to swipe right.

First of all, your profile pics should be brief snap shots of your life. They should be fun, exciting, and inviting to a woman. Women want to come across a profile and think, "hey this guy seems fun, attractive, and I want to see what else he is about" which will lead them to clicking on your bio, or even hitting the Like button on the spot. When choosing your pictures, keep in mind the attraction switches we discussed in chapter one. You should be focusing on showing those qualities in your photos.

Your first picture is your most important one. You must make it a picture that will grab the attention of the woman and lead her to wanting to check out the rest of your pictures. It is also important that this picture is of you, and only you. The last thing that you want is a girl clicking through the rest of your pictures only to discover that the guy that she liked in your first photo was actually not you. I will talk about group photos later in this chapter.

You want this first picture to accentuate some of your best qualities while conveying personality to the onlooker. Also, you want it to subtlety flip her attraction switches. The first picture on my current profiles is a scenic beach picture of myself, next to a famous rock landmark, on a vacation I had taken.

Email me at bradyPUA@gmail.com for examples of the pictures that I use!

The picture has only me in it, it is close enough to see my face, body type, style, but I am also not the only subject in the picture. The landmark shows that I did not take this picture only to upload one with my shirt off to be attractive. It shows that I look great, but I also have an adventurous side by making it to this landmark, which is not easy place go to. It also implies that I like to travel and experience new things, i.e. I am not a boring fuck. Also, it is not a selfie so it implies that someone else is with me as well, i.e. I have friends.

These are the qualities I like to convey in my first conversations with women online as well. I like to bring up travel quickly since I like to travel, and I like to convey that I am spontaneous and adventurous. I am not sitting around at home swiping and living a boring life. Instead, I am out busy, traveling to new places, and living my best life. A lot of times, I will open my phone to see new matches and women messaging me to ask where the landmark is that I went to. This is another great thing that you want your pictures to do: give the girls a reason to message you first.

I always think men should take the initiative and message first. It shows that you are confident and interesting based on what you end up messaging. Some women, however, will be attracted and will send you the first message. This is wonderful because it tells you that the woman has an above average interest level for you. These ladies are some of the easier conversations to have and turn into a date on the apps, so it is important to give them something to message you about with your pictures and bio. More on this is Chapter Three.

Remember, when choosing your pictures that actual picture quality is important. Do not upload grainy, blurry pictures of yourself as well as any picture that has been photoshopped to exaggerate your looks. The grainy pictures (ones that look like they were taken with an old ass Nokia phone) will come off as low value to a woman. Make sure they are clean, clear, and of great quality. Keep all social media filters to a minimum as well. If you have a gut and do not want to show it off, keep your shirt on in your pics. If you have a gut, but photoshop yourself with a six-pack, you are doing a big disservice to yourself. If you ever meet girls, they will expect a guy with a six-pack, and they will know that you lied. You will be instantly unattractive, and your value severely lowered in her eyes. This is a big no-no.

Your next four pictures (yes, I believe you should have a minimum of five pictures on your profile) are a little more lenient, but they should follow a set of guidelines that I have listed below. I give little examples as well as do's and don'ts for each one listed.

Choose a picture that shows you in action with a favorite hobby of yours. Do you like to ski? Are you an artist of some sorts? These types of pictures are important because of a few reasons. One, they show you doing something that you presumably know a lot about. A woman who likes to go to Broadway shows sees a picture of you outside of the musical Hamilton will automatically be drawn to that picture. She will be a little more intrigued to find out more about you and, if Broadway is an interest of yours as well, you will have a shit ton to talk about.

Also, this picture of you and your hobby will imply more qualities about yourself. You will come off as more attractive just because you are doing something. What is more intriguing in these two scenarios: a picture of you standing outside of a truck in a parking lot, OR a picture of you standing on the bed of a pickup truck, while unloading a couple of kayaks (one blue and one pink to imply a girl is with you) and someone taking a candid picture of that. See the difference? The action picture is more intriguing, and you should look to include an action picture of your hobby.

To add to this, any hobby of yours will qualify for this picture. You live every day on this Earth doing something! Can be anything you love! Add that to your pictures. Do you play videogames all day? Perfect, upload a picture of yourself being focused while sitting in your gaming chair with your gaming headset on and controller in your hand (have your friend take the picture). Put a funny caption in the picture saying, "Preventing World War III while you fucks are sitting in the quiet office all day". This picture shows your hobby and is funny as well. Also, it is hitting the Successful Risk Taking, hero type of attraction switch as well as the Leadership one.

Give it a try and if you cannot think of something, please email me and I would be happy to help with this. bradyPUA@gmail.com

You can have a group photo, but it should show you leading a situation and/or you with attractive women to trigger Pre-selection. I like group photos because they show your social intelligence. Show a picture of you and a group of guy friends where you are the focus. This will help to flip the Leadership attraction switch. One good example of this is a picture of me lining up a golf swing. The picture looks like I am teaching the guys around me proper technique when, in reality, we are simply drunk on the golf course and I am taking a swing. The power of the picture comes with what it implies though, that I am the center of attention around all these other guys; there must be something about me that will make other people want to be around me. These thoughts are what is going to drive attraction in the woman viewer.

Another group photo that you should have is one of you with women. Remember, the more attractive the woman the better. If you do not have any attractive female friends, no worries. Honestly, this can be a picture of you with your sister and her friends, cousins, or anyone else that is an attractive female. Sounds a little fucking creepy, but hear me out, the girl looking and swiping on your pictures is not going to know that is your family. She will take the picture at face value and think, "wow there is something about him that made that girl like him, I wonder what it is". That is all you need. Trigger that thought and you are golden.

Still creeped out by the family/cousin suggestion? Same. Just kidding, it is a decent technique, however if this is not an option for you either, you will need to venture a little further to create this picture. The beauty of this is that we always have cameras in our pockets now-a-days. Be on the lookout when you are in public! See a cute girl with a funny shirt? Ask to take a picture with her. Go to a sporting event and ask to take a picture with the cheerleaders. Be creative. Anything you can do to have a picture of yourself with a bunch of hot girls around you is key. This type of pictures will work wonders in driving attraction.

Another great photo idea is to have something artsy. If you tackled this well in your first photo then you can move onto the next suggestion, however having another like this is not a bad idea either. By artsy photo, I mean something with some depth to it. Something with an awesome landscape that will stimulate conversation. Ever been to the Grand Canyon? Upload the pic of you standing on a cliff.

I have a picture of me from a buddies wedding where I am standing in a pose similar to when Superman rips open his suit to reveal the Superman logo on his chest. I am revealing the same logo; however, the entire picture is black and white with only the Superman logo in full color. This picture was done by a professional photographer, but a few filters or YouTube videos later and you can create something like this as well. Ask a woman for help if you know one too. And be creative! Women will see this picture and open the conversation always with, "Are you Superman?". It is important to have an amazing response back to this as well.

Finally, almost as important as your first picture, be sure to have a picture that is funny! I try to be funny throughout all my pictures with a sarcastic tone as well. Your bio will help set this tone, however we will discuss that next chapter.

A funny picture can encompass a lot of things. I like to make the picture making fun of myself as well. One of the best examples I have seen of this is comedian Eric

Andre's picture of him taking a shit. The picture is as if someone opened the door on him while he is shitting and quickly snapped a picture.

This is great for a few reasons. One, it is funny. It's for sure to get a laugh as it seems everyone has had someone accidentally walk into the bathroom on them, which makes it a shared experience. Second, the moment of vulnerability being captured, and then willingly posted, shows that you do not give a fuck. This kind of attitude puts out a level of confidence that most guys do not have, online or in person. Also, most guys will not post a picture like this to a dating app, which is great for us. Remember, we want to stand out.

Third, when you boil it down, the picture is hardly embarrassing. Everyone shits and everyone has had that happen before. Some prude ladies may not like it, but whatever Eric Andre is not the type of person who would enjoy being with a prude girl anyway. More on this in the Part II conclusion.

A funny picture does not have to be embarrassing of course. I like the extra boost of confidence that women will apply to you from it, but a funny picture can be anything you think is funny. Can you turn yourself into a meme somehow? I did this when I went to London. I stood at what seems like the most popular phone booth, the one with Big Ben in the background, and I posed for a picture. The caption of that picture is "New phone, who dis?". This is great because I pretty much meme' d myself and now I use that picture any time I get a new girls phone number. That is the first message I send and it stands out because no one else has/sends shit like that. I made a meme out of it, I can send it as a joke, and the picture is also of me in another country which leads into the traveling theme of my profile. See how I tie it all in?

So, as shown in the above example, your picture does not need to be laughing on the floor funny. More like something new and refreshing that will put a smile on someone's face. The reaction that we want to have here is the "okay this guy seems interesting" reaction. This reaction on a couple of your pictures and you will be one large step closer to matching.

Do you have kid(s)? Use them! Be the best Dad in the world in your pictures. I do not have kids myself, but I would advise not to hide this fact. Also, do not make your pictures all about your kid(s). Still show the pictures that I have listed above but include your children in a couple of them and make sure your bio mentions them. This is a great opportunity to check off the Protector of Loved Ones and Willingness to Emote attraction switches. Men without kids can use one photo with a niece or nephew, or even your parents/grandparents, to convey these attraction switches.

I have pictures of my Mom and I on social media. The best thing about these pictures is that I am not the one who uploaded them, but I am tagged in them. Having someone else brag about you in photos that you are tagged in is extremely powerful. You are receiving whatever amazing quality they give you without having to say anything. It is also more believable to a stranger if it is coming from someone else.

I can tell a lady in conversation that I am the Worlds Greatest Son. Maybe she believes me a tad and we laugh about it. I could also direct that lady to my social media pages where, when she stalks me like she inevitably will, she will stumble upon a few sappy tagged posts of my Mom calling me the Worlds Greatest Son. See how the second scenario has more of a powerful effect on her? I now have that quality (Worlds Greatest Son) and I never actually had to say it. What you do not convey in your profile, or if you want to double-down on a few switches, use this method and you will notice how marvelous it works.

Another extremely important concept to use is to stimulate different emotions with your pictures. Women are far more in tune with their emotions than men are. They respond in a much more active way when their emotions are stimulated. Stimulate those positive emotions in your pictures and watch the matches and comments pile up.

I want to close this chapter by providing a summary list of do's and don'ts to think about when choosing the best pictures to upload.

Do:	Don't:
Use great quality photos that will stand out; use vibrant colors as well	Use grainy or old photos that have poor quality. DON'T PHOTOSHOP
Have a couple of common themes that you can use in conversation later	Be stale and/or lack personality
Poke fun at yourself, or dating in general	Insult or think you know more about women in general

Use photos that are taken from a lower angle, this will show height and masculinity	Use close-up, mugshot-like photos
Be humorous	Have the same type of picture multiple times
Show character and personality in your pictures	Use pictures that do not corelate to who you are as a person
Have a first picture that stands out	Use a shirtless mirror selfie. Even if you are in shape, show it in not such a bland way i.e. on a beach with babes
Have multiple pictures	Only have one picture
Use pictures that are serving a purpose to your overall profile	Have "filler" pictures or pictures up with no reason or story behind the,

Chapter Summary

Your pictures are the first part of you that someone will see when they come across your online dating profile. Make sure that they represent you to the fullest and they follow the guidelines I have provided above.

The first picture is your most important one by far. Make sure that it stands out and intrigues the woman to invest time in checking out your profile more. Do not make it a selfie or close-up face shot. Also, do not have any other people in your first picture. It should be of you and only you, but with a lot of personality as we discussed earlier.

In your other pictures, be sure to include a group photo that will check off attraction switches listed in chapter one. This picture should be checking off the Leadership and/or Pre-selection switches. A picture with an attractive woman, or a lot of attractive women all around you, will work wonders to increasing the amount of attention your profile will receive. Be sure to have this type of picture in your profile. If you do not have one, go to lengths to get one!

Use your kids, nieces/nephews, or parents/grandparents in a photo to convey the other attraction switch qualities. Even better if you can convey these based on other people's pictures on social media!

Be sure to review the Do's and Don'ts list above as well. Take the time to do it for every picture. This will only serve to ensure that you have given thought to each picture and will force you to take new ones to replace your old, shitty ones. Ultimately, we want to have every picture serving a purpose while checking off one or more of the attraction switches from Chapter One.

As I said before, pictures are the first part of You that someone will see on these dating apps. A guy who takes the time have the highest quality, highest personality and substance, and most meaning in his pictures is the guy who will be successful. Remember all the tips from above and come back to use this chapter as a reference when changing your pictures.

Chapter Three: Bio

Having a blank bio is easily one of the biggest mistakes to make on a dating app. Having a bio that stimulates no emotion from a female is as bad as having a blank bio. Your pictures intrigued her into reading more about you, now you want to waste her fucking time by telling her how you work for corporate America, like to cook, and you like music and sports. Wow, great fucking work Romeo, you must be drowning in women.

Quite the opposite actually. You are on zero dates and that is because you have zero emotions in your bio. This is your chance to continue showing your personality, humor, intelligence, sarcasm, whatever quality that defines you. This is also your chance to build your profile in a way that actually weeds out the wrong girls from swiping. As I stated above, I am not a fan of matching with a prudish type of girl so I make sure that my bio is not something they are looking for either. This helps me to attract only the hottest women that I know I will have the best times with.

As I stated in my intro to Part II, building the bio is my favorite part of the process. I enjoy it because you are creating a person, a character, before someone's eyes. Of course, this is a character of you, but here you can really boost yourself and accentuate your best qualities. I always look at my bio with some goals in mind: what am I looking for on this app currently (short-term fling, long-term girlfriend, etc) and what type of woman will fit what I am looking for? Am I looking just for a few friends with benefits? I will make sure I state that. Do I want to date a girl a bit before I fuck them? I will make sure my bio reflects that. Do I want to just attract as many high-quality women as possible? I use that as the goal in my head when I create my bio.

For the sake of this book, I am giving you tips on building your profile to attract as many high-quality women as possible, for as many dates as you can. If you want something different and want some tips, you buying this book has entitled you to that and you can email me at bradyPUA@gmail.com for questions.

There are some basic things that you should include in your bio, but this is only if you have these qualities to "show-off" I'd say. A lot of these basic things go back to the five attraction switches we discussed in Chapter One. Below is a list I have complied that show the simple things to include:

- If you are above 6ft, give your height

- Brush on some aspect of success in your life

- Say something no one else will say

- Give a hint of what you are looking for – Grounding Line

- Show Disinterest

Let's discuss each item on the above list and I will give tips on how to say them as well.

There is a big benefit to height in the dating and mating world. As you look at all couples, all over the world, you will notice a trend of the male being taller than the female. This is of course not a rule that cannot be broken or have acceptations, however it is an instinct built into a woman's head that goes back to our attraction switches.   The Leadership and Protector of Loved Ones switches are flipped (and your scores go up) subconsciously for any man who is taller than the woman. Because of this, it would be stupid if we do not convey such an easy quality if we have it.

Think about it, even as you are swiping and reading other girls bio, a lot of them will state their height. I see it a lot wrote as, "I'm 5'8' and I like wearing heels so you better be taller" or some other shit like that. This is a legit fear for women. They think that they will meet the guy and have him be shorter in person than they imagined.

Actually, I cannot count how many times I have met a girl for the first time and she has said, "wow, you're tall" (I am 6'3'ish). I can literally feel her joy as she realizes this, and it is an instant attraction switch flip in her head. I have also noticed that in times when I do not have my height listed in my bio, one of the questions I will be asked a lot is how tall I am. I was actually annoyed when I first started online dating because of how often it occurred, but it made sense when I thought about it. In person, women never need to ask this question because they can see your height. However, it does seem like a lot of women have been fooled on previous dates so they will be sure to ask about your height

Now, height is such a good attraction switch that this is one of the few qualities that can be listed as plainly as saying your height, 6'3'. However, since humor and sarcasm are qualities that I display throughout my profile, I will say my height in a sarcastic ass way. I currently have my bio saying, "I am 6'3', wow, you ladies really care that much? Weirdos.".

For me, this is the perfect way to convey my height while accomplishing many other goals at once. One, I am saying that I am tall, instant attraction switches flipped. Two, I throw in the sarcastic question, "you ladies really care that much?" which is great at conveying that a lot of women have asked me my height on this app (Pre-selection, if you haven't picked up on that yet, dip shit). Three, I finish with a "Weirdos" comment which can easily generate a bit of fun banter back and forth while adding a little to my Normal Emotion Programming score. Notice I am not calling them bitches or something more obscure. I am calling them weirdos which it could be easy for me to think they are weirdos because I am always being asked how tall I am. Most of the time, the comment is brushed off, but some women do use it to start a conversation. I discuss this more in Part Three of this masterpiece when we talk about what to say to women.

This sarcastic way of conveying your height is my route that I take. Again, use your common themes or best qualities to convey your height. If you are not really a sarcastic person, just say your height. If you want to be nerdy but funny, say I am you are 75 inches tall. If you want to be nerdy, funny, and sexual, say you are 75.6969 inches tall. The possibilities are endless, just make sure you are conveying your personality traits as well. Remember, we want to stimulate emotions.

Okay, finally, the part for all you short fucks out there. Yes, it is a disadvantage to being short. Here is how you get over it:

You have to own that shit. You must have the attitude of, "yes, I am short, who gives a fuck". This is the easiest way to convey that, while physically short, you have the personality of someone eight fucking feet. That display of confidence in yourself will negate any bad first impressions that a lady may have of you because you are not her ideal height.

This type of attitude and confidence can easily be portrayed in your profile. A comment such as, "5'6', but I wear heels too so you're good" or "5'6', and fucking loving it"

A few things to remember about your height if you are short: One, do not ever become defensive about it. **A man who is defensive is showing a weakness and/or insecurity which is two vibes you never want to give off to a woman.** Two, do not try to persuade or justify your height. Saying things to a woman like, "hey my height is average" does nothing to increase attraction in a woman. Instead, as I said earlier, you must own it. Take the mindset that you are tall. Your attitude and confidence are what will convey that, while you are physically short, you make up for it in a personality that even tall guys do not have. You're short. Fuck it. What can you do about? Tell the girl to take a second to get over the height thing while grab your booster seat. Be funny and nonchalant about it. Remember, her words don't affect you, you still know that you will show her a good time.

The next part of your bio I want to discuss is how to include some aspect of personal success. You want to do this subtlety as anything you say that is over the top here could come off as braggadocious. The purpose of having this line in your bio, like all others, is to convey personality and flip those attraction switches. Success in your life can check off the Leadership as well as the Successful Risk-Taking switches.

Again, as you come up with your own personal success line, be sure to use your personality in the line as well. Furthering my sarcasm and not-giving-a-shit attitude, I use the line, "Did you only swipe for the rock picture? I am college educated and have a career and shit too".

I am coming off as not really caring much to impress whoever is reading it. I am subtlety saying that I have success in my life while commenting that they probably only swiped on me for the shirtless rock picture that I have. I am telling them that there is more than meets the eye, and almost putting them down for only thinking I was attractive for my first picture. A line like this shows my successes without bragging about them, almost in a, "yeah, I have a good job, so what?". Often, an interested girl will flat out ask me what "college educated and shit" means. This is showing that she is interested! Always have a good response to say back when a girl shows this interest.

Also, women do not want to associate with a dead-beat guy who does not have a job or a bright future. Remember, they are doing value judgments in their head based on your profile. If you do not have a high-enough value for them, i.e. high attraction score, you will be swiped left on without hesitation.

Big confidence line here, listen up! The next line in your bio absolutely must be saying something that no other guy has in their bio. This line is going to provide some shock and awe value, a little bit of personality, and stand out to the reader. It will be the line that hooks your target into, not only swiping right, but giving them the energy and motivation to want to message you first.

Also, you need to make sure this is the third line in your listed in your bio. The reason you want this to be the third line is because of the comedic timing of the number three. The punch line in jokes always comes on the third line and we are going to use this to our advantage. This line does not necessarily have to be funny, just to provide that shock value that will pull the women in. Want to know what I use?

"I am probably shitting while reading your bio, sorry."

I chuckled out loud as I typed that again. It is something that we all do: using our phone in the bathroom. There is a chance that she is sitting on the toilet while reading your bio as well. It is an instant shock, laugh, and displays that "no fucks given" attitude that I carry throughout my pictures and bio. It also takes a level of confidence to put something like that in your bio and that is something women will be attracted to immediately. Not that you are shitting numb nuts, but the fact that you are brave enough to tell it to the world.

You want it to be almost a fear to put whatever you decide to put for this third line. It should violate social norms, but in a way that will draw mostly positive attention to yourself because of the confidence displayed.

Do not go overboard with this part. Some people do have an internal sick or twisted personality, but I would still avoid any line that has to do with negative emotions like anger, any kind of violence, or any sort of degrading commentary towards women. If there is any degrading, it should always be aimed playfully and at yourself. It's wild to me that I have to include this paragraph, but there are some wild fucks out there. Chill out bros and just have fun with this.

Some other great examples of a shock line would be:

- No hookups? I think you meant to dl Christian Mingle

- I already told my Mom about us

- Our President told me I can grab em by the pussy

The last one is political. Sometimes it is frowned upon depending on your views and what area of the country you are in. The point of the third line is to be polarizing, but in a way that agrees with your target. In some contexts, being political will fit. If you do not give a rats ass about politics, nor have any knowledge of the political views in the area you are in, I would not use a line like that. If you are knowledgeable and feel like you can use it to your advantage in your area, use it! It can be a powerful line when used correctly.

This fourth line you will use in your bio is what I like to call a grounding line. It is a line that pulls you back to Earth and gives a little more depth to yourself. It shows that after the crazy shit you just said, you are still on here for something.

The use of the grounding line is not all of the sudden changing positions or saying "just kidding". We want to give the impression that we are cool being ourselves but not wild all of the time. An easy way to do this is to give a hint of what we are really looking for. Say something here like, "It's Tinder, lighten up", or "How about we just grab some food and discuss why I need to watch You on Netflix", or "Is anyone down for casual drinks, don't like fucking if I barely know you". With a line like this, you give the woman a goal to work towards, having you take them out for drinks. This line also provides a bit of Disinterest, which leads to the next part of the bio.

Disinterest is an immensely important concept to have in your bio. Have you ever seen the movie American Hustle with Christian Bale? In this movie, Christian Bale's character is a con-man. One of his biggest techniques to hooking the mark to the con is to show disinterest.

Irving Rosenfeld: It's the crazy thing about people. The more you say no, the more they want in on something. It is so stupid.

Disinterest is a powerful tool to use in all aspects of persuasion and human psychology. Having a line that shows that disinterest will give the person a lack of what they want, which is for you to be interested in them. We all want what we can't have. If you give off the impression that you do not want them, that is also scarce as every other guy is trying hard to get them. Play it cool, have a disinterest line, and you will see success.

Also important to remember when discussing who we want to attract. Generally, a rule of thumb on dating apps is that there is a quantity vs quality battle. You can look for a lot of quick flings, but then you have to deal with a lower quality of the flings. You can also look for a higher-quality woman, but they usually do not operate as fast as flings do.

What I will teach you here is the best of both worlds. How to attract the as many high-quality women as possible while making sure that your bio will cut down on the pretenders, time wasters, or any other types of women you will not be attracted to. I will also teach you a little about what to look for when swiping and how to avoid the fucking bots that are rampant on some sites.

The last thing we need to touch on in your bio, is your use of spelling/grammar as well as emojis. You must ensure that your spelling and grammar are all used properly. The last thing that you want to have is a sarcastic, snarky ass bio that is full of misspellings and grammar issues. A woman will call you out on this for sure, that is if she even swipes in the first place. Showing unintelligence is unattractive. Be sure to proofread your bio, check your spelling, and make sure you are using the correct versions of your/you're, their/there/they're, and seen/saw just name a few of the most common ones.

Chapter Summary

Having and profile that stands out amongst the rest will surely get you more matches. Women will aimlessly swipe through hundreds of loser guy profiles on a weekend. You need to make sure that your bio is the one that excites her and flips her attraction switches. You want her to swipe right!

Remember that when building your profile to have those attraction switches from Part I of the book in mind. Also, run through the lists of Do's and Don'ts I provided above to make sure you are not committing any common, loser guy mistakes. Have Pre-selection pictures, have the attention-grabbing statement third in your bio. Do these things and you will surely see more matches ASAP.

Be sure to use your bio and pictures to weed out any women that you do not want to attract. I personally steer away from prudish women because I know that I will not generally fit well with them.

Also, have fun with it! Try out new shit. Say new things and note down the positive or negative responses from it. Update your pictures and accordingly to ensure that you have the best content to represent you and have the most matches.

Important notes before moving on

One of the best parts of having these dating apps right in your pocket is the ability to change your pictures and bio almost immediately. This is great for trial and error. When you start making changes to your profile using the suggestions in this book, you will find that some things work immediately, and others will take some tweaks. When you start receiving complements on certain pictures or aspects in your bio, be sure to keep those! The pictures or bio lines that are not receiving as many laughs, questions, or attention, be sure to some up with something new and update your pictures/bio. This will help to keep your content fresh and exciting, as well as it will come up in the feed that your content has been updated. This will lead to more exposure to previous matches that may have flaked on you before.

Earlier in Chapter Two, we were discussing the picture of Eric Andre shitting and I said the line, "Some prude ladies may not like it, but whatever Eric Andre is not the type of person who would enjoy being with a prude girl anyway". To me, this line sums up some important underlying themes of this book.

I have matched with, met with, and slept with hundreds of women from dating apps. All have had different personalities and traits; however, one of the things that they almost all had in common were they were not ultimately extremely prudish or religious types. A lot of women pretend to be prudish at first, but that is more because of the Madonna-whore complex (Google Madonna-whore complex for more information). This basically states that women come off as being a prude at first because a woman who shows too much of her inner desires will be considered a whore, while the prude is more respected as wholesome. Once you are good at game, you can identify which woman who is a prude, and which is a pretender, and make sure that you are in the pants of those pretenders. More on that in later books.

To complete my Eric Andre reference above, I am not the type of guy who would waste time trying to match and connect with a woman who is an actual prude. I personally do not have anything negative to say about a prudish woman, however it is not something I am interested in. I, like Eric Andre would, build my profile to weed out the prudes. There is not much of a chance that this type of girl will see my profile and want to match with me, which is completely fine with me! I do not want to waste my, or her, time to figure out that we will not be a good match.

You should build your profile in this way. As I said, nothing wrong with being a prude, it is not my type though. Maybe it is your type and you should build your profile to attract a more prudish type of woman.

The beauty of all of this is, all women have the same attraction switches! All the advice in this book will hold up regardless of the type of lady you are attracting. Now put it to good use, make those changes, and start meeting women!

PART III: What to Say

"It's not harder to get a 9 or a 10, it's just different" – Mystery

I think this is the part of the book a lot of readers are looking for. Sure, building a bio helps to get more matches, which is surely something you want, but I feel like a lot of guys struggle with what to actually say. At least I know I used to!

When I first started my journey from an Average Frustrated Chump to a Pick-up Artist, What to Say was the topic I was most interested in. I had a decent number of matches but it seemed like my openers and basic conversation would have little responses and interest back to me. I felt like I could generate a lot of interest from 6s and 7s, but not much interest from the 9s and 10s which is the category of women that I truly wanted.

It took me a while, lots of studying and trying out new material, before I realized that you can attract those 9s and 10s easily. You have to use material that is geared towards that class of women. You can walk up to a 7 or 8 and complement her but you just can't do that to a 10. Also, 9s and 10s would altar my state, as in, I knew that I really wanted to fuck these girls so I became more nervous and not myself. I became outcome dependent, which is focusing too much on what I really want out to the situation, and that is to fuck that girl. This outcome dependent state is telegraphed to the lady through your words and body language too.

Don't think a girl can tell this shit? Think about it. A girl who is a 9 or 10 knows she is beautiful, and she most likely has average chumps telling her this every time she steps out of her house. Women in general have a good detective-like instinct of figuring out a guy's true intentions pretty quick and it is usually stronger on a higher-valued target. If you say and do the things that all other guys say to her, she will put you in that category of all other guys and now you are lost in the shuffle of thousands of other guys who just want to fuck her too. Lost forever.

We need to make sure that you are standing out. You are not like those other guys. In fact, you demonstrated pretty quick that you are different. Your bio is funny and mysterious, and now its time to demonstrate that you can back it up with your words. Part III will instruct you on how to transition ladies from the app to more direct forms of communication, all with great communication skills.

Chapter Four: Rules

Before we discuss wording and content of messages, I want to lay some ground rules down for *how* to message. These are important because following each of these rules will ensure that you do not run out of shit to say, ensure each message you send has a purpose, and ensure that you are flipping those ever-so-important attraction switches.

Below is the list of rules and I follow them up after with further description and reasoning behind them. Be sure to understand why each rule is a rule and why they should always be obeyed.

Rules:

1. Always message first

2. Follow, then create the conversations pace

3. Use proper messaging size

4. Use proper spelling and grammar

5. Continue to escalate

Always message first

You must always message first. This rule is in place for quite a few reasons. One, it is generally expected for the male to message first. This is a super easy way to flip that Leadership attraction switch as well, so fucking

use it. Two, a lot of women will not message first anyway.
Since this is the case, what the fuck good is a match if you
are not even going to start a conversation. A match with no
conversation is not much different that no match. Every
match is a start, a lead, and a shit-ton of potential for new
conversations, new fun, and overall experience. Send the
damn message!

Also, use this first message to draw the woman in
more. Women are constantly testing men to see if they will
display congruence. At this point in their head, you are
exhibiting a lot of attractive traits. You have the intriguing
pictures, they were pulled in by your bio, and now you
have to back that behavior up with stimulation
conversation. You start that process by sending that
amazing first message.

Some dating apps require the woman to message
first. I am not a fan of this because most first messages are
copy and pasted messages, or simple messages like "Hey".
I prefer messaging first and displaying those wonderful
characteristics right in your first message to display that
you are, in fact, that intriguing person represented in your
bio.

A lot of times we will be messaged first because our
bios are going to entice that, which is great. In situations
where we are messaged first, we will have some choices on
our responses that I discuss more in Chapter Five on
Opening. For now, just know that your ass should always
be sending the first messages.

Follow, then create the conversations pace

This rule is all about the old-school rule of waiting 30-minutes before texting or responding. The thing about the waiting 30-minute rule is that it is kind of accurate. The last thing you want to do is come off as too needy and eager with conversations. Trust me, I have fucked myself over quite a few times before because I have been too eager to talk. It seems from being outcome dependent; you want to hook the girl, so you just regurgitate a bunch of lines and respond too quickly. Remember, you are strangers talking. Even though she is gorgeous in her pictures you still have no idea about her and you need to maintain that attitude.

Also, not only does responding too quickly come off as needy, which is fucking annoying to a woman, it shows that your life is boring and that you have nothing going on. Would Brad Pitt or Leonardo DiCaprio be constantly texting the same girl and messaging back immediately? No. That caliber of guy would have plenty of options, and plenty of busy shit going on. They are scarce and anything that is scarce is instantly a higher value. That is human nature. Make your messages intriguing, but scarce as well.

Now this does not mean to not message, nor does it mean to wait forever to message. Remember, you are a busy guy with an important life. However, what I follow is this:

After you open, see how long it took her to respond. I would always wait at least 30 minutes. Also, your second and third messages should be somewhat sporadic. Maye you respond in 10 minutes, then your next message in the conversation is two hours later.

Here is the kicker to all of this, a little concept I like to call **conversation momentum**.

Conversation momentum is the shortening of time between messages due to two or more people having a conversation. This is such an important messaging concept and will lead you to numbers a lot faster than waiting the 30 minutes or two hours to message. Do not ever stymie a conversation because you could lose out on the girl as well. If you have momentum built, keep going until you have her number!

Here is an example of what I mean by conversation momentum. You open your dating app and notice that you matched with a girl last night. It is noon now and you send the first message. She replies at 1:30pm. You see that she replies at 1:30pm, but here is where you should wait at least 30 minutes to send your next message. You respond back at 2pm.

Maybe this girl has a typical 9am – 5pm daytime job. In this case you would respond casually as she responds, mimicking the same amount of time it takes her to respond to the first few messages. If she waits an hour, you also wait close to an hour. This is you following her pace at first. It makes her feel like you are busy, and it does not trigger her alarms that you are needy or low value.

This is a good starting conversation structure, but soon you are going to want to respond a lot quicker to her to generate momentum. This is you generating the pace of the conversation and taking the driver set, leading role. Find a time that she would most likely be able to respond quickly back to you. Following this example, it should be right around 7pm – 9pm at night when she is home from work, gym, dinner, etc.

The idea is that you respond quick at a time she is most free, and she will respond quick back to you. Pretty soon, you are messaging each other back as soon as the other one responds. Congrats! Your bitch-ass is now having a conversation with a girl!

Seriously though, this is such a powerful tool to use. Quick conversation like this can build you massive amounts of attraction in a short period of time. This will guarantee a girl to even give her number to you without you giving yours.

To be honest with you, once I have this type of conversation momentum, I know that my chances of getting this girl go up significantly. Follow the process in the rest of this book and you will have the same results as me, guaranteed. There are peak times in the day for conversation momentum to happen as well. You can judge this for yourself and structure when you reply to incite conversation momentum to happen.

The important thing to remember here is that you do not want to stymie the conversation from ever happening. Get the momentum and roll with it. If she is active on the app and not talking to you, it is because she is talking to your competition. Do not let yourself lose the girl because you are waiting 30 minutes to reply every time.

Use proper messaging size

Proper messaging size is important when you are generating conversation momentum or keeping the conversation rolling. Think about it, if you start the conversation with a huge monolog all in one paragraph, chances are the girl will not read it. She will open, see a big blue paragraph, and then ignore it and skip to her next match/message.

Also, if you ask a lot of questions all at once or tell too long of a story, chances are you will not be sent a response back. The reason is, even though it would only take a minute to read your message, the girl looks at your large message as a large investment that she is not ready to make into a stranger. It will require her reading it all and/or answering all your questions, which is not worthy of her investment back.

Yet, at least. Some can be ready to invest that kind of time into a stranger on an app, and even more so if you have a great profile that is intriguing, however chances are the only response she would send back is a short, one-line response, if any at all.

Also, long messages show you are investing a lot into a stranger, which can come off as needy. As I have said before needy is the last way you want to come off to a girl. It is so fucking unattractive to them so it's a big no-no from the start.

You need to make sure you are baiting the girl to invest in your messages. Part of this is also in your message language. Women are stimulated with emotional language. The easiest way to ensure you are embedding emotional language in your messages is to be sure to use the work "because" in your sentences. Do not just tell her that you like football. Tell her that you like football *because* it is the one thing that you and your Dad always bonded over, or whatever emotional story you can attach to it. Use this in your messages, and for sure use this shit in real life. It works.

Use proper grammar and spelling

This is admittedly a pet peeve of mine. When I am being messaged, it is a turn off to be talked to in an uneducated way. If everything is shorthand and text speak, sometimes I will choose not to respond.

The above paragraph is actually a quote from a girl (super hot) describing how important proper grammar and spelling is. Remember, you want to come off as high value. Coming off as uneducated to a woman is a sign of lower value a lot of times. There are messages that I shorten with conjunctions and such, but I always use proper spelling and grammar.

I do not correct girls if they message me with a few mistakes here and there because I do not want the conversation to be about me being the grammar police and such. I do, however, make sure that I am using proper grammar and spelling myself and I correct myself if I make an error. Again, this makes you come off as educated and of a higher value. Show that you can hold a conversation.

Continue to escalate

When you are messaging a girl on a dating app, keep in mind of your ultimate goal: to meet her in real life. Everything that you build say and do on the app should be to work toward this goal. In order to achieve this, you need to continue to lead and escalate your interactions.

By "escalate" I mean that you should keep moving the interaction forward through a predictable sequence of events. I have had sex with a girl from the app without having her phone number before, however this is extremely rare. To meet the girl in real life, you are most likely going to need her phone number and/or social media accounts. These will be your other mediums of contact and the preferred methods as well.

I always go for a girl's number first. You will know when the feeling is right to go for the number. It is usually when your conversation momentum is at its highest. This is an easy transition right from the app to text messaging without skipping a beat and has a high percentage rate for success.

Also, you are going to want extra insurance that she is real too. Sure, setting up a meeting right from the app is spontaneous and exciting, however it is also dangerous and nerve-racking. Because of this, I always do things to verify the girl is real and that she does look like her pictures (more on this in Chapter Five). The easiest ways to verify she is real is to get her phone number, social media accounts, etc. This is the purpose of escalating.

Chapter Summary

There are rules that you must keep in mind when you are messaging a girl. Although there are sometimes caveats, these rules should always be followed.

Remember to show your leadership skills and message first. Even if the girl messages first, you need to take control and lead the conversation with the things you say. You can do this with the timing of your messages, as well as having intriguing content in your messages (more on this in the next chapter).

Use proper messaging size to avoid coming off as too needy, or too much of an investment to the girl. If she has to read a lot and type a lot back, that is seen as a large investment of her valuable time into a stranger. You need to make sure you are not investing too much of your own time into her. Also, be sure that your spelling and grammar make you sound educated and of high-value than someone using slang and text abbreviations all of the time.

Continue to escalate with the girl. A lot of that will come naturally as you gain more experience, however use the conversation momentum to your advantage. I have slept with a lot of women in the same day I met them online because I escalated when the momentum was the highest.

Chapter Five: Opening

Finally, the chapter you have all been waiting for. Let's talk about what to say to these girls to have them wanting to meet with you in no time.

I have tried hundreds of different openers on dating apps. They range from the simple, "Hey, I'm Cody, nice to meet you" to the "Lets bang" and I have had failures and success with all of them. The important thing to remember when opening is what you ultimately want out of talking to that girl. Do you want quick sex? Do you want to take her out? Decide what you want and then tailor your opener to reflect that.

Also, remember with the goal of opening is: to have a message sent back to you. That is it. You are opening just to be sent a reply. A reply is the ticket to having the rest of the conversation.

Also note, if a woman does not reply to your opener, you are allowed one follow-up opener and that is it. If that is not replied to, simply ignore the conversation. A lot of guys will unmatch at this point, which I do not because I do not know that specific girls' situation. Maybe she got back with her ex-boyfriend, but maybe that will only last a week where they break-up she logs back onto the app and sees your message. This has happened to me before.

Above all, be sure to not harass these girls or be fucking creepy. There are a ton of weirdos out there and it makes life hard on women, and our lives harder because their defenses are raised higher. Be creepy and I will fucking come find you and hurt you. Promise.

Quick Sex

A lot of what I want was to simply have sex with them. This can be achieved by using a direct, "lets bang" type of opener, however the success rate is small. An opener like that only really works on women who:

1. Are on the app just to have sex as well

2. Feel attracted to you from your profile

This is most likely a small percentage of women you have matched with, so this is not the ideal opener for all women that you match with. You should only use a direct sex opener when the profile of the woman is direct as well. Something like, "Here for a good time, not a long time" will compel me to send the direct sex opener. I mean, why waste time with all of that other shit?! She is here for a good time, we matched so she liked my profile, now it is time to bang. Pretty simple, right?

Sometimes it is that simple.   I always leave room for error with it, so I make my direct sex opener a little more high-value than "lets bang". This is because you are surely not the only guy she matched with and other guys are probably messaging her the same thing. If she is going to pick one of you to sleep with, we need to make sure she pics you.

Again, you do this by making your opener higher value. You need to make yourself stick out, while also not coming off as a dirty-type of guy with possible STDs and shit. In order to look for the quick fuck, but portray higher value, I use something like this:

"Hey Emma"

"Today was one hell of a day in the office. Would you be down for some causal, no strings attached sex? You're super cute and it would be fun. If you are down let me know, but if not, no worries! □"

With this method, I am going straight to the point. I open with her name to throw off the idea that I am sending the same message to all girls, which sometimes I am. Regardless if I am or not, this message give the perfect vibe in my opinion and has worked a countless number of times for me. I am being straight-forward, confident, and coming off as non-needy with the "no worries" line. Also, I give off the impression that I am asking because the day was a great day, or a stressful one. It is open to their interpretation, so it leaves wiggle room to make sure you are not too high above, or below, her energy level. They are either having a good day too and hopefully they read it as such, or their day is stressed too and they could use sex to help.

If you do not want to be as ambiguous with your opening line, I suggest that you always come off as positive and in a good mood. This is almost a rule actually; however, you never want to be too high on a level that is not where the girl is. It can come off as too eager and needy. With practice, you will have the feel of how to come across.

One of the last things to know about the quick sex opener is that if it does not hook, you are most likely done with that set. I have successfully rebounded being turned down during the quick sex opener and had relationships from it. This is advanced and hard to do. For now, imagine that if you shoot the quick sex routine and it does not work, you shoot any other chance with the girl as well.

General openings

We covered the rules and the Quick Sex opener, now we need to cover what you will be using almost all the time, the general opener.

General openers for me have to be short, personable, and stick out to a girl. The simplest opener out there that I would ever use is two quick messages:

"Hey Jenna (girl with hand up emoji)"

"I'm Cody, nice to meet you"

That is the simplest opener I would ever use, and I will be honest, it is not that good. However, this opener is relying on the fact that your profile is off the fucking charts awesome, so I will most likely receive a "hey" back. That is all that is needed though for me to continue my demonstrations of higher value.

To add more to this opener and make it better, I would add in some observational piece regarding the girl's pictures or bio. For example, if she has on a red lipstick in a few of her pictures, you can say something like

"Hey Jenna (girl with hand up emoji)"

"I'm Cody, nice to meet you. Shit, you are the queen of red lipstick"

But you can add in anything there. Try to find a commonality too. If you both have cool landscape pictures, say, "I'm Cody, nice to meet you. Shit, we are the King and Queen of badass landscape pictures". With a line like this, you are standing out and making yourselves fictional royalty. Role play is always fun with a girl, remember that.

Another successful way to start the conversation is with some role playing where you are conducting an interview. This is fun because since a lot of guys will ask basic interview questions to a girl. You essentially take that idea and make fun of it to show that you are different than those guys and to convey that you talk to a lot of women so you know how to talk and you are not boring as fuck. A way to start this opener would be:

"Hey Jenna (girl with hand up emoji)"

"I'm currently accepting applications for a (insert the upcoming season) adventure partner"

"The pay is shit, but the benefits are amazing. You should apply"

This opener is one that a girl will not receive often, if ever. That is good because it will stick out more as well. Also, it is simple like the others, not too many words that requires a lot of investment back from the woman, and it is versatile in that you can move in so many directions with it. It has a sexual element as well so a woman who reads it in a sexual mind state can comment back like, "mmm, tell me more about these benefits". This will lead you right into your other routines that have even more of a sexual element to them. I talk more about routines in the next few sections.

Chapter Summary

Be the one to open first. Open the conversation with an opener that fits with your intentions. Sometimes a girl is only looking for quick sex so be sure to recognize this and open appropriately if this is something you are also interested in.

Use an opener that has the girls name and possibly something about her profile. This will eliminate the feeling of it being a copy and pasted opener. If the lady does open you first, be sure to take the lease in the conversation after that.

An opener should be versatile and intriguing of some sort to hook your target. The purpose of the opener is to receive a response back and start the conversation. If you open and have no response back, it is okay to send another message after some time, but do not bombard the girl.

Once you have a response, congrats the conversation is successfully opened! Move to the next phase which is using your routines and DHVs.

Chapter Six: Routines and DHVs

In this chapter I will cover more of that actual content on the messages that you will send. I give you techniques that I follow in every single conversation I have with a woman. We will talk about using canned routines (copy and paste messages that you use over and over again) and how to make sure they are embedded with DHVs (demonstrations of higher value). I include a couple of effective routines that I use and I also talk about how to create your own routines. Finally, I close out this chapter with how to keep the conversation escalating by using the Number Close effectively. This will ensure that we are not stalling out the conversation or only creating new social media friends/followers. We want real results from this so that will always be our goal. Enjoy!

Routines

Just to be clear, hopefully this section is an overview similar to Chapter One on the various attraction switches. If you are unfamiliar with routines, please check out my book

Routines are going to be the epitome of your success when it comes to figuring out what to say to a woman. They are going to help you tremendously. After you open successfully, you are going to use some canned routines to get the conversation going. Routines are what will help you never run out of shit to say.

Have you ever watched stand-up comedy? Think about your favorite one, or the most recent one you watched. A comic stands on stage and tells funny stories. They use the right sound effects, jokes, pauses, banter with the audience all at the right time in their stories to entertain you. You watch and you laugh.

This is the exact same concept when using routines to talk to women. When comics tell jokes, they are not making them up right on the spot. They travel around saying essentially the same jokes from city to city. They practice the timing, wording, emotion, etc, of every joke they tell until it is perfect and they have the audience laughing every time. This is all a part of their act; their comedy *routine*.

Of course, when you are having a conversation with a person it is not as structured as this. However, when chatting with women on a dating app (or in real life), you will use the same concept of routines. You will practice them with all of your matches and, once they are perfect, you will have the experience to know when to use them and how to use them to escalate.

I provide a few routines in the following sections. There are also an abundant amount of proven routines that you can find on the internet, as well as on my sites and shit. More importantly, once you start to have more experience with game, you will be able to develop your own routines. I have come up with mine just with various random conversations or funny things that have happened in my life. I have perfected them and use them regularly to build attraction online and on dates. With a little practice, you will have a full arsenal of proven routines as well.

Your opener is the first routine that you use. We discussed this in the previous chapter. After you successfully open, you are going to want to use a routine to transition into the conversation you use. I always try to keep this first transition consistent with my opener. For example, if I use an opener that is specific to a girls profile at all, I will make sure that I follow up with a routine that is along the same lines with however I opened. Also, this transition routine should be relatively short. Remember, we do not want to bombard her with overly worded paragraphs and lots of message up front. We want to ease into the conversation casually.

For example, I have the Job Interview opener (discussed in Chapter Five) that I use often. If I open with it, I will use the Benefits routine after. Below is my Benefits routine and then an example of how I would use it:

Benefits Routine

Well, talking to me does have its benefits.

1. I will visit dog parks and rename all of the dogs to whatever I want.

2. I am really good at making PowerPoints with slide transitions and word art and shit

3. Tandem Halloween costumes. I am the topless fireman and we light you on fire so I can spray you with the hose and put you out. Tons of fun for sure

Haha, I am kidding of course. What were you last Halloween anyway?

I use this routine in my messages because it is so diverse. It is humorous and you can ask a number of questions in the end depending on the lady. Does she have a dog in her pics? Name it (don't ask about it, just name it). Is she in school? Tell her you will build her next presentation for a small fee. And of course, the Halloween question.

When you are using this routine after the opener though, you need to shorten it. You can't send all of those messages at once, it is too much initial investment and not genuine. You would use it as a transition routine like this:

"Hey Jenna"

"I am currently accepting applications for a Summer adventure partner. The pay is shit but the benefits are amazing actually"

"I think you should apply"

"haha, okay what are the benefits"

Or

"Hi Brady, okay lol"

"1. I will visit dog parks and rename all of the dogs to whatever I want.

2. I am really good at making PowerPoints with slide transitions and word art and shit

what can you offer?"

See how I shortened it a bit? You will want to do the same thing when you use a routine as a transition routine. Again, this is just to keep investment levels small for now so we can gradually raise them over time as we continue to DHV.

Demonstrate higher value

Remember, women are attracted to someone who has value. Even more attracted if that value is higher than theirs. Values are perceived attributes that can be attained by flipping the attraction switches we discussed in Chapter One. We can flip these switches when we have a conversation with a woman by demonstrating that we have those values in the ideas and manners in which we talk, and in what we talk about. Everything that we have discussed so far has been for the purpose of starting the conversation. Now that we have the conversation successfully opened and transitioned, we are ready to demonstrate higher value (DHV).

When we have a conversation on the dating app (successfully matched, opened, and we have a response) we are going to give small personal stories that will check off her attraction switches. These are our routines. Forget always trying to make conversation based on her pictures or her bio. We will allude to that for sure, but if she has a picture of a dog, do not say "Oh nice dog, what's its name?" A good rule of thumb for having a conversation is to take whatever the first thing you would normally say and throw that shit out to the trash. If she has a picture of her and a dog, do you think every other fucking guy has asked about her dog already? Yes. So don't ask. The same goes for tattoos or any other identifying qualities in her pics or bio.

"But Brady, she put a picture of her in a kayak, she must like kayaking. I like kayaking too. Why can't I talk about that?"

Because you are no longer the same as the ten other lame guys who asked her about kayaking today. Everyone loves kayaking, don't bring it up.

There is a line here to think about as well. Commonalties can be strong attraction builders so if you two have the exact same type of dog, or heaven forbid the exact same tattoo or some shit, you can talk about this. But the consensus is that if it is something you would normally say or mention, don't say it! We want to be saying and talking about shit that she has never heard. This is especially true for the 9s and 10s because a lot of them do not want or need to be on dating apps anyway. Anything you can do to differentiate yourself from the other lame ass guys is a plus.

Below I provide two more routines that I use often. These are app tested and always generate a positive response and attraction. After the routines I provide a small summary of what exactly I am attempting to convey and what attraction switches I am looking to flip. Make sure to keep all of that in mind when you are building your own routines. I am dedicating a whole book to building routines so if you need more help with this be sure to check it out when it is complete.

Travel Routine

> *Brady: If you could travel to any where in the world, where would you go and why?*

Jenna: I have always wanted to go to Bahamas for the beach.

Brady: Yeah, I have been and it's amazing! The island food is actually underrated, it is not on many food shows but it is awesome. I am all about food when I travel. My list is to go back to Europe to eat authentic pasta in Japan, hope of to Japan for the freshest sushi, then finish in Turkey with a big ass turkey sandwich.

Brady: With like avocado. Gotta be so good there right?! Whole country named after it.

Jenna: haha sounds amazing! Not sure if that is a thing though

For me, this routine is doing a few things. One, it is showing that I potentially have enough resources in my life to do expensive things like travel the world. I am also displaying some humor and personality while finding out about her a bit. Some girls love to travel and have big aspirations of the countries they want to visit. In this case, Jenna is more of a typical or basic girl who only wants to go somewhere warm for the beach, or at least this is what she is showing me so far. I can judge her levels of interest and stuff from her smaller, less enthused response. Also, if she is more enthused, you are bringing up good memories of some trips she took. Those memories will trigger positive emotional responses in her, which she will attribute to you and your conversation.

The best thing that I like about this routine is that the versatility is endless. If the girl responds more positively to the travel question (longer response) you can roll with that. If you have been there before then that is a good commonality. You can transition into the food topic (everyone loves food) or you can transition into any other short story possible that DHVs.

Even when you are not using a canned routine, you need to still make sure that you are DHV'ing with everything you say. You can flip her attraction switches in pretty much everything you say. For example, she asks a basic question like "how are you". You never respond by just saying "good". My typical response will always have DHVs built in. Here is an example of my programmed response to "How are you?":

"I'm good! The office is pretty relaxed today. Just killed a meeting I was prepping all morning for and I am surprising my niece for her birthday later. She's turning 7 and so adorable. Her party is at the Zoo, which I haven't been to in ages."

I included things in my conversation that will flip her attraction switches. Leading a meeting successfully at my career and being excited to see my niece later. Showing my Leadership abilities as well as my Protector of Loved Ones qualities. Notice how I mentioned them casually as well? I am not coming off as bragging but answering her question genuinely.

This response also provides many different paths the conversation can travel down. It gives her many different topics that she can inquire about next and allow you to circle back to one of the topics to make sure you are never running out of shit to talk about. She can ask about what I do for work, the last time she was at the Zoo, how many nieces/nephews that I have, what I got her for her birthday, etc. Maybe later that night or in a few days, whenever the conversation gains more momentum, you can talk about how much fun you had at the Zoo or how the meeting you lead successfully got you some amazing recognition at work. You do not have to lie either, you can be vague. Amazing recognition does not necessarily mean a promotion, maybe a higher up told you "good job". That could fall in the limits of great recognition.

Use emotional language

Women respond in conversation when you stimulate their emotions in some sort. This is one of the biggest techniques I use whenever I hold a conversation with a woman, not just through text, but also in real life. Below, I provide you with the single biggest trick to use when you are talking to a woman to ensure you are using emotional language.

The word "because" is one of the strongest words to use to a woman. You should be injecting this word into your conversations and routines as much as you can. This word will allow you to put emotion into virtually every sentence and make you so much more interesting of a person. It will almost guarantee you are using emotional language, which is what you need to do in order to hold the attention of a woman. They are emotional creatures so you have to use emotional languages (unlike men who have more logical brains) in order to stimulate their minds. Let me demonstrate this with a couple of different sentences.

"I like World of Warcraft." Seemingly perfect sentences to convey a like to a logical brain. However, when talking to women, I would use the below sentence instead.

"I like World of Warcraft because it is the one time during the week when my close buddies can set aside time to get together and we all just have a blast playing and catching up"

The sentence provides more context and you can inject more emotion in that sentence. You can use this with any and every topic as well.

Move to other communication

Now you are having a conversation and you are DHV'ing up the ass. She is responding positively and you are having great conversation momentum and flow. At this point, if you have all of this, you are ready for a fucking phone number close bro! Congrats!

The number close is simple, but really effective when you use it with the right DHV's. For starter, you need to remember that you are a man, a leader, pre-selected, etc, and you need to formulate every message and response as such. If you believe you are high-value, trust me, you are and your messages will come off that way as well.

"Hey, we have been having good conversation and I think that I want your number so we could text"

"Hey, I do not use this much so could I have your number and I can text you?"

FAIL. WRONG. LAME-ASS.

Do any of those above messages sound like a guy who has his shit together? A guy who is high value? No!

When we number close we never ask for a number. That is step one. We also never come across as wishy-washy, timid, shy, any of that. We are men. We need to be assertive, strong, and concise.

"Actually, I want you to have this. 555-555-5555"

"Here, I'd love if you texted me."

Okay these are not bad if the conversation is good and she is an 8 or below. If she is a 9 or 10, we need to qualify her a bit. Make it seem like you are unsure about her at first, but she is winning you over somewhat. For a 9 or a 10, you would use something like:

"You are actually a decent person to talk to. Here, just don't request a dick pic, or get your ass blocked! Lol 555-555-5555"

Something short, simple, and you never ask for her number. You always have to give yours out. I like the addition of the "dick pic" and "get your ass blocked" line to show that this has possibly happened to you before. You are coming from an abundance of women so of course girls would want to see your dick. Just another slight DHV embedded in your number close. You want to use something like that for the hotter girls, but also not the same thing verbatim if you are talking to a more prudish type of girl. Remember to recognize your type and use the words that she would respond to more. Trigger those emotions as well!

Sometimes, girls can still be iffy on if they want to text you. Don't take this as a rejection! Maybe the douche before you called her non-stop and stalked her so now she is being more cautious about who she gives her number to. Because of this, some girls will ask for social media first.

Here is where it can be a little tricky. I like the number close because it is more of a direct line of communication between you and the girl. Also, we are going to use the phone to demonstrate major confidence in Part V of this book. Some girls (usually the hot ones) are only on dating apps to increase their social media followers. Genius actually, what chump would not add a hot girl if she is freely giving out her social media. She increases her followers and he thinks he somehow has a chance. But he doesn't and she knows this. You have to be on the lookout for a situation like this which is why I always continue to escalate to am actual phone number.

I have settled for snapchats before phone numbers because this gives the girl, and you, a few more ways to build attraction off of the app, but more personable. You and her also have the ability to see what the other one actually looks like, or what their lives are like before you invest further. Also, it is similar to text now the way you can chat back and forth. Again, just be careful here that you are not talking to someone who is only looking for more followers.

Below I have a checklist of the things to look for before you know it is cool to ask for a number. Once you have the feel, this will become second hand to you. You will know when to use the number close.

- Back and forth conversation

- At least 7-10 messages sent

- Indicators of interest from the woman

- She is not trying to plug her social media

Even after receiving her phone number, which is the preferred method, you should still do a little sleuthing on social media. You are not going to outright stalk her. You are not going to try to add or message her on there unless you have been invited to, and you are not going to leave any kind of likes or comments on any of her pictures/posts/etc. Read those lines again and fucking memorize them please. Go ahead, I'll wait.

Yes, we do want to do a tad of looking her up on social media; however, this is only to confirm that she is a real person and confirm she looks like how she advertised. We want to make sure she is real because there are catfishes and fake accounts out there. You never want to invest time into someone who is not actually real. This does happen and it can be heartbreaking. Look up Manti Teo's story.

We also want to confirm that she looks like what she advertised. I do not see this much, and when I do it is more with guys giving the false narrative, however women can for sure use angles and filters in their profile pictures to make them appear different than how they really look. For this reason, I advise men and women to do some social media looking up beforehand. If for whatever reason you cannot find them on social media, no worries. In the next section of the book we will discuss more ways to verify they are real.

Investment

An important thing to discuss before we close Part IV of the book is the concept of Investment. I have mentioned investment a couple of times previously when talking about how we should not be sending long, bombarding messages at first. They should be short, and sweet, and intriguing. This is because investment level between two people is something that is increased gradually, in small amounts, over a period of time.

Think about it like this: you match with a girl, is the first message you send her about how badly you want to fuck her? No! However, in a few weeks or months of talking/dating, could that be an appropriate message to send her? Yep. It is because you have been talking and dating, there is a much higher level of investment she has in you. We must build that investment up over time.

If you give her your number in the first message, will she text you? Chances are no. If you talk with her for a few messages, get to know each other more and then give her your number will she text you? Chances are yep! And high chances as well.

We need to be starting small and gradually building investment over time. Gradually increasing her attraction will also increase her investment. We need to be careful not to try to increase attraction too quick as well as this is usually unnatural and could give off uneasy feelings. You can do this, but then she will attach the player vibe to you which may not be something you want if you are looking for something longer-term. We never want any negative feelings to arise in a woman when we are interacting with her.

Chapter Summary

Remember that you should be using Demonstrations of Higher Value to flip those attraction switches when having a conversation with a woman. The easiest way to do this is by using stored Routines that you have perfected over time.

A routine is good routine if it can increase your value in a woman's eyes while also stimulating her emotions. Use emotional language and the work "because" to ensure that you are appealing to her emotions. Also, you routines should provide many different topics of conversation so a girl can respond to one at that time and then you can refer back to a topic that was not completed at a later time. This will ensure that you never run out of things to say when in conversation.

Be sure to always escalate the communication to phone texting and social media. This will provide you more momentum leading all the way to the date. Also, it provides you assurance that you are talking to a real person, who is who she says she is.

Start with smaller routines and then increase them gradually. You do not want to scare her off by sending her big blocks of messages or asking for too much at once. Starting smaller will gradually increase the investment a woman is willing to make in you. Making out with you immediately when you meet is a big investment. Making out, and more, after you have been dating for a few months is no longer a big investment. See what I mean?

PART IV: Setting Up the Date

Here we are, the final part of the process. This is the last little bit of game we play to secure that we can meet this girl in person. By now we should have generated a lot of interest and attraction as well as weeding out the girls that we would be unattracted to. Finally, this is the part where we separate ourselves from the other guys she is currently texting and secure our date in her schedule.

In Part IV, we are going to cover the basic concepts of text game as well as talk about how to build huge attraction quickly and how to keep that momentum rolling until you meet. I will cover the one thing that you will absolutely need to do to ensure that you stick out from any other guys she may have recently met. You want to be different from them, so we must do different things. We will ensure that we are showing massive amounts of confidence and value at every step.

We will finish by closing with the date setup and making sure we keep the momentum moving until it is date day. This will help to cut down on the number of flakes, especially if there is a long wait before the time where both of you are free for the date.

Chapter Seven: Text Game

At this point, we were able to generate high conversational momentum and strategically number closed when it was at its peak. Congrats! You have a new phone number to add, a new contact in your life, and soon a new love interest. What we need to do now is follow a similar pattern of routines and DHV'ing until we have enough conversation momentum to setup the date. We will use some of the additional features of texting (picture messaging, calling/facetime) to continue to convey our confidence.

Opening the text conversation

You gave your number out on tinder and dundumdun! A text message comes across your phone. Maybe: Jenna. Fuck yeah!

When we start our text conversation, you can do a few things. If the conversation online was already turning sexual or towards meeting up faster than usual (same-day date), you need to keep this momentum going! Don't stall out the conversation just because you want to wait 30 minutes before replying. If the replies are coming back instantly and there is good chemistry, keep right going to the next section of the book about FaceTiming.

If not, we need to imagine that the conversation momentum that we had on the dating app is now slightly lowered, or that a new bar is in its place. Instead of this momentum bar starting at Dating App and ending at Phone

Number, this new bar starts at Phone Number and ends at Date. We need to build the momentum back up until she is now read to set a date to meet in person.

We open this conversation with something small and simple, similar to the dating app open. There is one difference here though that can generate a lot of attraction: we can send pictures. This is exactly what we will do too.

No, this is not a time to send dick pics. I believe there is hardly a correct time to send dick pics. If a girl wants to see it, she can see it in person. Otherwise, it is just her games that she is playing.

We need to continue to convey confidence. The firs thing that I do is send a picture of myself to the girl. There is a catch, this is not just a random picture of my face and this is definitely not a picture that I already have on the dating app. Instead, I send her a picture of me, standing in a phone booth in London with a caption that says, "New phone, who dis?"

This particular picture is perfect for me and fits immediately with the situation. One, the girl just texted a random number. The picture is confusing at first: did she text the wrong number? She double checks it, nope. Did I just ghost her? I time my next text about a minute after I send the first one. "Haha, just kidding, its Cody". I generated a lot of different emotions in her with my first two texts. Great start.

Also, this picture goes with a lot of the routines I would have already discussed with her. I like to travel, I like to joke around (sense of humor is social intelligence which is attractive), and now I have sent her an unsolicited picture that was not a dick pic. I am already better than the fucking creeps who send their dicks right away. Why would a girl even want to receive that anyway?

I recommend that you follow this same practice as me. You need to find a picture that will convey your personality and go along with the themes that you have already presented her.   You need to show congruence with her. You built up all this attraction by talking the talk, now you need to display that further. I talked about how much I love to travel and such and now she has a picture of me in an entirely different country, just as I said I like to do. See how it makes me seem more genuine? She will think, hmm this guy isn't just a bullshitter.

This picture requirement is hard to provide generic examples for because everyone is different. You will need to think on your own to come up with something that fits you; however, I am always available for additional help at my email, bradyPUA@gmail.com.

Fucking FaceTime her

This is one of the most powerful displays of confidence that you can do after starting the text conversation. I have had countless women tell me that they thought is was super attractive. I used to actually be nervous to FaceTime, but now that I have done it so many times and I have the setup for it perfected, it is one of my favorite parts of this process. If we can have a successful FaceTime call, I know my chances for the date are exponentially higher. This does not mean that this part is required for the date, however this will almost guarantee it in my opinion.

Also, the FaceTime call provides much more familiarity with each other. This will help massively to have her want to meet you in person. You will have a better idea of what you both look like, you will be familiar with each others voice, and FaceTime gives the other a glimpse of your environment. That being said, make sure your environment is clean and stimulating when you FaceTime. Do not be somewhere dirty, don't be topless, and don't be somewhere with a poor connection as this will stymie the call.

After you open her with the picture opener through text, you are going to want to find the exact time to facetime her. I always try to make this happen on the same day you get the number to keep the conversation momentum going. By now, just through basic conversation, you should have a good idea of what type of schedule she has. If she has an office job you are not going to FaceTime her at 2pm on a weekday. Instead, wait until 7pm at night to start the FaceTime routine. You can also ask her generally what she is up to. If she is out with friends, or at the gym, or doing something that would make it tough for her to answer a FaceTime call, you should not try to FaceTime her yet. If she seems mostly free, execute the FaceTime routine!

The FaceTime routine is simple. As you are gaining some conversation momentum through text, you are going to simply ask her "Are you ready for your test?". Her response does not matter much. If she seems free, you wait a minute or two after she responds, and FaceTime her! Simple as that. From here, the conversation can go a few ways.

She answers your call and you two start a conversation. In this case, use some of the routines that you have in your arsenal and also, circle back to stories that you two have messaged about before. This would be things such as how was your niece's birthday party or how was the zoo. Also, there are things that come up when I message a girl that I will make a mental note to bring up when I run the FaceTime routine. A lot of times these are things too long to text like if a girl asks me about the topic of the book I am writing. I can bring that topic back up and explain it more over the call. All while DHV'ing up the ass of course.

I always try to make these calls around ten minutes long, tops. You are not there to build all of the attraction, you only want to demonstrate your confidence and make her familiar with you. This will increase how much she wants to invest in you. Always be sure that you are the one that ends the call. I try to do this at the height of the conversation. Right after you say something funny and have her smiling, tell her that okay it was great to talk and that she passed your test, but that you have to go for the evening. After you talk, give it about 30 minutes and text her that you had a great conversation. I always try to allude back to the height of the conversation and have another laugh about it if possible. Even tease her maybe. This will lead you right into asking when she is free for the date.

She does not answer your call. Most of the times, this is still as powerful as if she did answer and you had an amazing conversation. The reason this is still powerful is because you just put her on her toes, you made her a little nervous, but in a good way. You did something that guys hardly ever do and you made her more intrigued. The reason she did not answer, in my experience, is because you actually surprised her and she was not expecting that. Her makeup is not ready for it, the lighting is not showing her good side, all things like that. She wants to make a good first impression too! And the good news is, you just made your good first impression. You are confident, you are not scared to have an easy chat with her. All of this shows in your FaceTime attempt, I promise you.

If she does not answer, again this could be for endless reasons, don't take it as rejection. Know that you just did something that only 1% of guys will do. I simply send the text after that says, "FAIL". I then send the text, "What, are you not wearing makeup? It's okay I am not wearing any either" as a joke to her. She will provide whatever excuse she has and then maybe ask you to call back in 5. Regardless of how it goes from here, just know you impressed her.

A few caveats to this routine. If you do not have an iPhone you will not be able to FaceTime. You can use Snapchat and Facebook as well because they have FaceTime-like features. Make sure you set it up with her before hand as in, have her already as a friend on Snap/Facebook and message her if she is ready for her test on there. Also, all these techniques will work with a basic phone call as well. Instead of Facetiming, you can simply call her, however FaceTime is the one that displays a shit ton of confidence.

If she does not answer, the surprise is up, but be sure to setup the call for another time. Maybe the FaceTime was too much of an investment for her at the time. Warm her up over the next few hours, or days, and try to give her a call randomly. This will work to still display that you are a confident man and put you in that 1% of guys.

Set up the date

After the successful FaceTime call, you should have built a lot of attraction, comfort, and rapport with the girl. By this point, she should be wanting to meet you in person. This is the next logical step in this dating game as well. Some girls are confident and will come out and ask when you can meet up. A lot of girls will be subtle and give hints about her free time hoping that you will suggest the two of you meet up for a date.

Personally, I have done this enough times to *feel* when there is enough attraction and connection to ask for the date. This is a super power that you will eventually have as well once you have more experience (the same as when to know a girl wants to kiss!). When I feel this, I start to schedule the date right then and there. It is also usually best to ask when your conversations are at their peak. This usually occurs right after a successful FaceTime call but these peaks can also occur when texting as well.

What we need to cover is **how** to ask for the date. This is done much like the rest of the escalation steps we have taken so far (opening, getting the number, etc) which means we ask to go on a date with confidence and certainty. You can simply ask, "Hey, want to meet up sometime?", however I am always injecting additional confidences when I make these types of requests.

Start out with a question to gather when she will be free within the next couple of days. I always try to make the date within a week because it is easy for conversations to stall out if there is longer of a break between you agreeing to go out and your actual go out date. This can lead to flaky behavior.

Ask the girl, "I am sort of packed, but when are you free within the next few days?" She will respond with her free times. I always lead with a statement of being somewhat busy too. This is to make sure that I am not coming off as needy or too eager to see her. Also, it shows her again that I am a busy person which is congruent with my persona that I have displayed to her so far.

If she responds that she is not really free, tell her that you are also jam-packed this week but you were deciding if you wanted to do all of it or not. Then ask her what days she is usually the freest. If she gives a negative response again, saying that she is not free anytime soon, we may be asking to meet up with her too early and she will need you to build more attraction and DHV more before you try to date again. More on how to deal with this scenario later in this chapter.

Once you have the days she is free, pick one and be assertive. Do not ask to hang, use the words, "I want". So, to ask properly, it is not "Do you want to get together?". Instead, say "I want to get together on Friday. I will plan something fun and chill for us." This will convey that same confidence that you should have been displaying for the rest of your conversation as well. Also, it is a huge pet peeve for a girl to have to plan everything so that brings me to my next point.

Always have a plan for the first date! You need to make the plans and you need to set them up. This is all a part of you being the leader. Also, I stray away from typical date ideas and I always go for something more unconventional. The second date can be the more conventional dinner one, however, the first date should be a simple meet-up. I have done walks in the park, playing catch, walking dogs, little bars for a drink or two, checking out new parts of the city, etc. I keep them light and causal so there is no pressure on either party to endure a two-hour dinner date when there is no chemistry or things like that.

The point is to be the leader and plan the date, then show her some simple aspect of your life. I take a girl out for a drink, and then I walk her around my office building downtown. If she is more sporty, I take her to play catch, bringing two mitts, or I take her electronic scooter riding. The benefits of something like this is that it is more casual, which saves you expensive dinner-date money, and it is more fun that just sitting there interviewing each other for hours at a fancy restaurant.

The lady will do pretty much anything if she does not have to plan it. So many times, a guy will pick her up, look at her, then say, "so what do you want to do?". This can be frustrating as fuck and show that you are not manly to the girl. This also brings up the question of should you pick her up?

If you are meeting for the first time, I will sometimes offer to pick her up depending on what the activities I have planned, but I usually tell her to be at a desired location and at a time. This helps her to not feel trapped with a stranger as woman sometimes can and you never want her to feel uncomfortable. I use this method if it is the first meet. Every date after that, however, will be me offering to pick her up. Again, this is the leader qualities that you are displaying. Always be thinking of flipping those attraction switches!

Dealing with flakiness, or slowing communication

If this situation occurs, I will befriend her on some aspect of social media from her and make sure to post interesting stories. These can indirectly build attraction. I always try to post attraction building stories, however that is another subject that I cover more in further books and posts. I will also keep texting and building attraction just as if the conversation momentum bar started all over again. Schedule a few phone call dates with her as well.

If you two stop talking, or if she stops responding, do not overly chase! This is bad and comes off as needy and stalkerish. You never ever want a woman to feel these vibes from you. If you do, I will come kick your ass. Threat and a promise.

Always be talking to multiple women and never be just hooked on the outcome of one. This is something that will take some experience to desensitize yourself, however it is an insanely huge self-esteem boost when you feel this. This will increase the strength of your game as well because it gives you the non-needy attitude that is super attractive to women. Also, it is not the end of the world if you lose out on one attractive girl. Trust me, there are so many out there and as soon as one is out of the picture, I promise another one will come strolling in as long as you continue your approaching.

Chapter Summary/Key Takeaways

Remember to maintain your confident behaviors and your leadership qualities at all times. Sure you can take her suggestions into account, but be the decider and lead your interactions.

Keep imagining that momentum bar resetting at each new step. Continue to build it up by using your routines and DHVs to flip her attraction switches. When you reach the peak of the conversation, escalate it to the next step. Keep doing this, and you will soon have her number, her schedule, and soon on a date with her.

Do not feel rejected over one girl and never be only talking to one girl. Maintain the appearance of abundance and an abundant amount of woman will come to you. Take the leader role in every step: Opening the text, Facetiming, Setting up the date. Use the same characteristics that you have been conveying to ensure that you are being congruent i.e. maintain your goofiness or your humor if this is what you have displayed before.

Above all, have fun! You are meeting someone new and attractive, be excited about this!

Epilogue/Conclusion

I want to close out this book with some of the biggest tips I can provide from my experience. These are things that I always remind myself of and are a big factor in my successes.

Tips:

- Never be outcome driven

- Never be focused on one single girl (Oneitis)

- Never need the girl

- Always have fun

- Always have the mindset that she likes you

- Always display confidence and be leading

- Keep approaching and opening

- Keep learning and improving

- Keep learning about topics other than pick-up to widen your views

- Help others out who are struggling

- Help yourself by stepping out of your comfort zone

- Strive to be the best

Here's the thing: I want you to see results and I want you to share those results with me. Follow all of the tips and guides in this book, however, please email me with any part of this that you are struggling with. I want to hear everything! Your positives and your negatives, and I want to help!

Your journey with me does not end here. Please email me and stay in touch. I appreciate each and every one of you and I will do my best to respond and help with every question emailed to me. I greatly thank you and I am excited for this next part of your life to begin. Now go and fucking meet some women!

Acknowledgments

Thank you to Mystery, Style, Lovedrop, Seventy-Seven, Everyone's favorite Wing-woman Marni Kinrys, and RSD Max for your inspirational knowledge and stories.

And to all of the women out there I have had the absolute pleasure of interacting with.

About the Author

Brady is a self-proclaimed Pick-Up Artist who has been instructing other men in the art of Online Game as well as Day/Night Game since 2015. His biggest influences on the topic of Seduction are Mystery, Seventy-Seven, as well as RSD Max.

Working as a word-of-mouth guru in his own area, Brady has been successfully leading men to gain more and more confidence with women throughout the past five years. He has recently decided to increase his audience base by posting in Seduction forums, starting his own blog, and writing a book detailing his overall goal of seducing at lease one new woman a week. Check out more of his material at www.bradyPUA.com